Proposals for Peace Creation in East Asia In Cooperation with ASEAN

SHII Kazuo
Chair, Central Committee
Japanese Communist Party
April 17, 2024

Greetings and welcome, everyone. I am SHII Kazuo of the Japanese Communist Party. I would like to express my heartfelt gratitude to all the guests from embassies in Japan and from various fields of society, and all of you who are watching this live webcast from across Japan.

In East Asia, where we live, economic, human, and cultural exchanges have developed, interdependence has strengthened, and the general populaces of the region are eagerly seeking stability and peace. At the same time, there are various conflicts, tensions and confrontations as the rivalry between major powers intensifies.

How do we create an East Asia free of the fear of war? If we counter military power with military power, we will create a vicious cycle of distrust and fear, and create the danger of war, which no one wants. We need to pursue the possibilities of diplomacy to the fullest extent and devote ourselves to peace creation through diplomacy. From this standpoint, I would like to present a diplomatic proposal from the Japanese Communist Party titled "Proposals for Peace Creation in East Asia — in Cooperation with ASEAN."

First Proposal : Work with ASEAN to foster frameworks for regional cooperation for peace on an East Asian widescale

The first proposal is to work with the Association of Southeast Asian Nations (ASEAN) to foster frameworks for regional cooperation for peace in East Asia.

Great Hope for Peace Learning from ASEAN Initiatives

Dramatic shift from "division and hostility" to "peace and cooperation"

The great hope for peace lies in the efforts already made by ASEAN.

In 1976, ASEAN concluded the Treaty of Amity and Cooperation in Southeast Asia

Indonesia

Chair Shii meets with Mr. Ekkaphab Phanthavong, ASEAN Deputy Secreaty-General, at the ASEAN Headquaters in Jakarta on December 21, 2023.

Chair Shii meets with Amb. Adam M. Tugio, Advisor to the Foreign Minister of Indonesia, in Jakarta on December 20, 2023.

Chair Shii and Vice Chair TAMURA Tomoko (at that time) meet with Dr. N. Hassan Wirajuda, Former Foreign Minister of Indonesia, in Jakarta on December 21, 2023.

(TAC), which pledged the renunciation of use of force and the pursuit of the peaceful settlement of disputes. On the basis of this treaty, ASEAN has made persistent efforts for dialogue and dramatically transformed the region, which half a century ago was dominated by "division and hostility," into one of "peace and cooperation."

Since the late 1990s, JCP delegations have repeatedly visited Southeast Asian countries and witnessed the changes taking place in the region, which could be called a "decisive move for peace." Most recently, last December, we visited Indonesia, Laos, and Vietnam where we were able to witness the latest achievements of ASEAN's efforts and learn from the wisdom of establishing the mechanisms for regional peacemaking.

ASEAN is said to be one of the "most successful regional organizations in the world." What is the secret of its success? I would like to share four points that we learned from a series of exchanges of views during our visit to Southeast Asia at the end of last year.

They have nurtured a good "habit of dialogue"

The first is that they have developed a good "habit of dialogue."

When we visited the ASEAN headquarters in Jakarta, we were surprised to learn that ASEAN holds as many as 1,500 meetings a year in the region. With such a high density of meetings, mutual understanding and trust building can be promoted, and even if disputes arise, they do not lead to war. They also said that dialogue is a by-product of diversity. The countries of Southeast Asia are rich in diversity in every aspect, including in economic development, political systems, religions, and ethnic groups, and dialogue is thus indispensable in promoting mutual understanding.

It was emphasized that the "step-by-step"

Proposals for Peace Creation in East Asia
In Cooperation with ASEAN

SHII Kazuo

Japan Press Service

Japanese Communist Party Central Committee Chair Shii Kazuo on April 17, 2024 at a policy speech event held in the First House of Representative members' office building presented a diplomatic proposal titled, "Proposal for Peace Creation in East Asia – In Cooperation with ASEAN."

Proposals for Peace Creation in East Asia
In Cooperation with ASEAN

Contents

approach is being taken to solve problems in a feasible step-by-step way through dialogue. It was also emphasized that the decision-making made by consensus is the critical principle of ASEAN, with both large and small countries being equal and respectful of each other.

It is noteworthy that ASEAN has thus, step by step, fostered trust and transformed the region into a peaceful community through a long and persistent dialogue based on mutual respect and trust.

"ASEAN Centrality" — Value independence and unity

The second is to maintain the "ASEAN Centrality," in which they value independence and unity.

How does ASEAN view its relations with the major powers outside the region? When we asked, the answer was, "We welcome the involvement of major powers, but we do not take sides. ASEAN's independence and neutrality, with ASEAN always in the "driver's seat," has created a convening power in ASEAN and has served as a guarantee of unity among ASEAN member countries. This has attracted other major powers from outside the region, which are increasingly seeking to strengthen their ties with ASEAN. An expert we met said, "ASEAN has a convening power that can make countries with even opposing positions feel comfortable working out issues together."

Although the Southeast Asian region also faces difficult challenges, such as the South China Sea issue, and there are moves to divide member countries, it is important to note that ASEAN has maintained its "centrality" and unity by placing importance on the UN Convention on the Law of the Sea and inter-national law, and by exercising patience and flexibility.

ASEAN has been working on peace creation, economic cooperation, and social and cultural cooperation in an integrated manner

Third, ASEAN has worked on peace creation, economic cooperation, and social and cultural cooperation in an integrated manner.

During the exchange of views, it was repeatedly emphasized, "we need peace and stability for prosperity." The slogan of the Japanese small and medium-sized merchants' organizations — the Minsho and Zenshoren — is "Peace is the key to prosperity," and I felt that the spirit of ASEAN is the same.

At its 2015 Summit, ASEAN declared the establishment of the ASEAN Community, consisting of the Political-Security Community, the Economic Community, and the Socio-Cultural Community, and has been making efforts to deepen integration.

They have extended the trend of regional cooperation for peace beyond the ASEAN region

Fourth, this trend of regional cooperation for peace has been extended beyond the ASEAN region.

They emphasized, "for ensuring peace in Southeast Asia, peace in Northeast Asia and other countries outside the region is indispensable."

In 2005, ASEAN established the East Asia Summit (EAS) with the 10 ASEAN members plus 6 other members — Japan, China, South Korea, India, Australia, and New Zealand. The EAS was later joined by the United States

East Asia Summit
（EAS）
10＋8 countries

Japan　China　Korea　U.S.A.

Russia　Australia　New Zealand　India

ASEAN
（Association of Southeast Asian Nations）
10 countries

Indonesia　Malaysia　Philippines　Singapore

Thailand　Brunei Darussalam　Myanmar　Vietnam

Lao PDR　Cambodia

and Russia in 2011, and has now grown into a forum led by the leaders of the 18 participating countries to promote dialogue and cooperation with the aim of "promoting peace, stability, and economic prosperity in East Asia."

Concurrent with this movement, ASEAN has been making efforts to accept countries outside the region to accede the Treaty of Amity and Cooperation in Southeast Asia (TAC). This movement has spread in the 21st century, and the number of countries that have acceded the TAC has now expanded to 53 countries and 1 regional organization on a global scale, with its first meeting of the Conference of the Parties planned to be held in 2024.

Pioneering role toward a "world without nuclear weapons"

As a political party of the A-bombed nation, we have always been encouraged by the positive role played by ASEAN in working for the abolition of nuclear weapons, and since the establishment of the Southeast Asian Nuclear-Weapon-Free Zone Treaty in 1995, ASEAN has continued to lobby for the nuclear weapon states to sign the protocol. Many ASEAN countries have also played a pioneering role in the establishment and entry into force of the Treaty on Prohibition of Nuclear Weapons.

Today, ASEAN has become a major source of world peace. I believe that there is much diplomatic wisdom to be learned there.

Latest Achievement — The ASEAN Outlook on Indo-Pacific (AOIP) Initiative

The latest achievement in this effort to extend the trend of regional cooperation for peace beyond the region is the ASEAN Outlook on Indo-Pacific (AOIP), adopted at the 2019

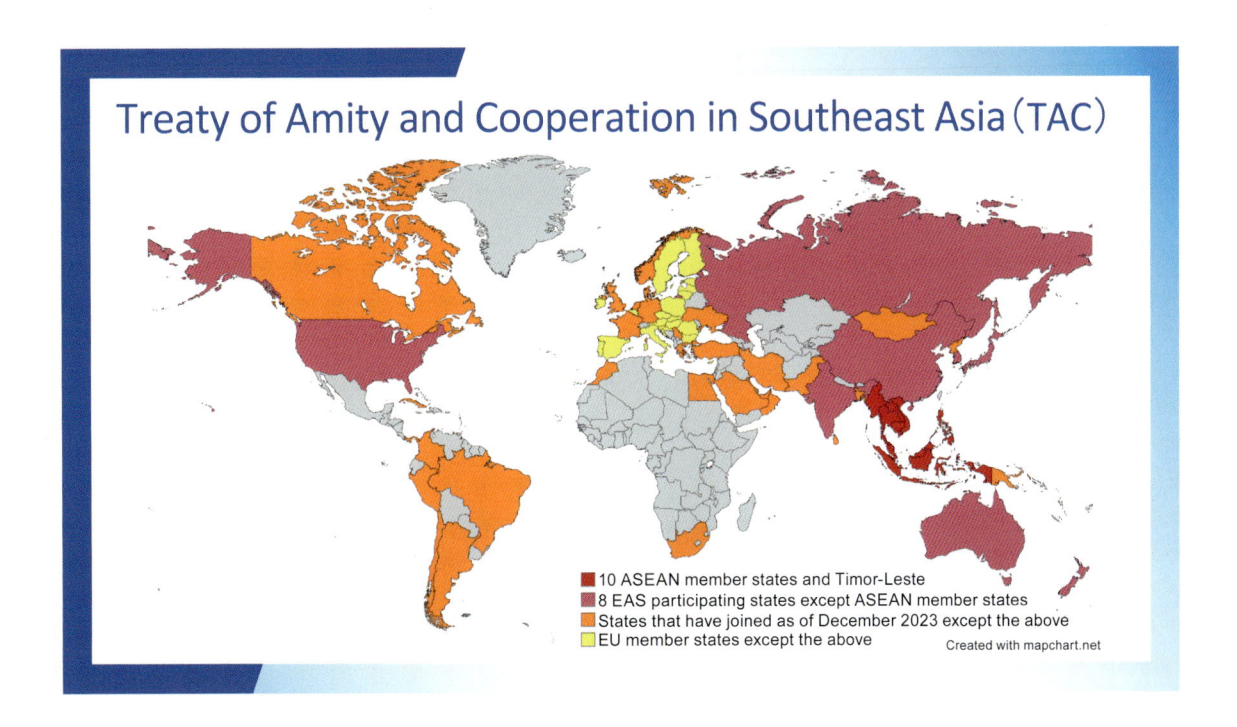

Treaty of Amity and Cooperation in Southeast Asia (TAC)

- 10 ASEAN member states and Timor-Leste
- 8 EAS participating states except ASEAN member states
- States that have joined as of December 2023 except the above
- EU member states except the above

Created with mapchart.net

ASEAN Summit. The AOIP is outlined below.

> *Create an Indo-Pacific region of dialogue and cooperation instead of rivalry, and focus on development and prosperity.*
>
> *Use and strengthen the existing frameworks, such as the East Asia Summit (EAS), as a platform for dialogue and cooperation.*
>
> *Utilize the Treaty of Amity and Cooperation in Southeast Asia (TAC), which stipulates peaceful settlement of disputes, as a guideline for peace, and promote it throughout East Asia.*
>
> *Promote the four areas of cooperation include maritime cooperation, connectivity including people-to-people exchanges, the UN SDGs, economic cooperation and others.*

The AOIP is a grand vision to extend the regional community of peace that ASEAN has achieved in Southeast Asia to all of East Asia. It has, in our understanding, the following important features.

First, they utilize the TAC as a guideline for peace, extended it to relations among nations throughout East Asia, while building prosperity together through practical cooperation in four areas. They have made these efforts simultaneously, so to speak, as "both wings" of practice.

Second, it aims to develop as an inclusive framework that embraces and includes all countries in the region rather than excluding certain countries.

Third, rather than creating a new framework, it is a realistic plan to utilize and strengthen the current existing frameworks such as the East Asia Summit (EAS).

Thus, the AOIP has become a common undertaking of the East Asia Summit (EAS) participating countries by taking a pragmatic and rational approach while setting ambitious

ASEAN-Outlook on the Indo-Pacific (AOIP)

- Create an Indo-Pacific region of dialogue, cooperation, development and prosperity, instead of rivalry.

- Utilize and strengthen existing frameworks such as the East Asia Summit (EAS) as a platform for dialogue and cooperation.

- The TAC, which stipulates the peaceful resolution of disputes, should be used as a guideline for peace and promoted in East Asia as a whole.

- Promote cooperation in four areas, including maritime cooperation, connectivity, UN SDGs, and economic cooperation.

goals. Joint statements promoting AOIP has already been adopted by ASEAN and most of the EAS countries, and the September 2023 EAS Joint Leaders' Statement clearly stated, "[the EAS leaders] support ASEAN's continuous efforts on the mainstreaming and implementation of the AOIP." The JCP believes that this statement shows the proper path to create peace in East Asia.

Proposal of JCP's "Diplomatic Vision" to Create Peace in East Asia

In light of the new development of ASEAN's advocacy of the ASEAN Outlook on Indo-Pacific (AOIP) Initiative, the JCP proposed the following "diplomatic vision" for creating peace in East Asia at the party's new year greeting speech in January 2022, and has been working hard at home and abroad to realize this vision.

> *What Japan needs to do now is not to expand its military build-up, but to engage in diplomacy that makes the most of Article 9 of the Constitution in order to make East Asia a war-free region by joining hands with ASEAN countries, setting the realization of the ASEAN Outlook on Indo-Pacific (AOIP) Initiative as a common goal, and utilizing and developing the East Asia Summit which has already been established.*

The "Diplomatic Vision" of our party, which I have just introduced, has the following characteristics.

First, it offers a peaceful counterproposal for Japan's security. A security policy that focuses exclusively on strengthening military responses will lead to a vicious cycle of military-to-military confrontation, which in turn risks threatening the peace and stability of the region and Japan. The "Diplomatic Vision" is to create peace in East Asia through peaceful means, centering on diplomacy.

Second, the "Diplomatic Vision" is not only a proposal for Japan's path forward, but also an international call by a Japanese political party to work together to create a framework for peace that is inclusive of all countries in the region, rather than excluding any one country, with the goal of realizing the ASEAN Outlook on Indo-Pacific (AOIP).

Third, the Diplomatic Vision is a proposal based on the spirit of the permanent pacifism stipulated in the Constitution of Japan and Article 9 of the Constitution of Japan. The ASEAN spirit to promote cooperation for regional peace can be summarized as follows — "Disputes may be inevitable in human society, but it is possible, through the wisdom of all peoples, to prevent conflict from turning into war." This is the very spirit of Article 9 of the Constitution of Japan.

Actions at home and abroad to realize the Diplomatic Vision

The Japanese Communist Party (JCP) has been taking action both inside and outside Japan to realize its "Diplomatic Vision."

At the International Conference of Asian Political Parties in Istanbul, Turkey

In November 2022, our party sent a delegation to the 11th General Assembly of the International Conference of Asian Political Parties (ICAPP) held in Istanbul, Turkey — an international conference attended by 69 political parties from 31 Asian countries — to appeal for support for the AOIP. We also called for the creation of a framework for peace in East Asia that is inclusive rather than exclusive, a central tenet of our "Diplomatic Vision."

International Conference of Asian Political Parties (ICAPP)

Chair Shii speaks at the 11th General Assembly of the International Conference of Asian Political Parties (ICAPP) in Istanbul on November 18, 2022.

The Istanbul Declaration, unanimously adopted by the General Assembly, clearly states that ICAPP will "stressed the importance of avoiding bloc politics and emphasized cooperation over competition." "Avoiding bloc politics" means to "not take exclusive measures." ICAPP has developed as a forum for peace open to all legitimate parties operating in Asia, regardless of ideological differences. The Istanbul Declaration signifies that the direction of our "Diplomatic Vision" has obtained consensus in the conference by political parties in Asia.

The 7th Congress of the European Left Party in Vienna, Austria

In December 2022, our party sent a delegation to the 7th Congress of the European Left Party held in Vienna, Austria. In our remarks, we stressed the importance of AOIP and introduced the "Istanbul Declaration" adopted by ICAPP, emphasizing, "This is a significant voice from Asia at a time when there are strong concerns about the trend toward opposing blocs in the world." Representatives from European countries, where the bloc confrontation and division by NATO and Russia are worsening, expressed their strong welcome, saying, "It is wonderful to know that there is a practice in this world that opposes bloc politics and is moving to create peace with an inclusive conception of all nations participating."

Visit Three Southeast Asian countries — Indonesia, Laos, and Vietnam

Our party's "Diplomatic Vision" was well received and welcomed during our visit to three Southeast Asian countries in December 2023.

In an exchange of views held at the ASEAN headquarters in Indonesia, the response was

Congress of the European Left Party

JCP Vice Chair OGATA Yasuo makes a speech as a guest at the 7th Congress of the European Left Party in Vienna on December 10, 2022.

Lao PDR and Vietnam

Chair Shii meets with Dr. Thongloun Sisoulith, General Secretary of the Lao People's Revolutionary Party and President of the Lao People's Democratic Republic, in Vientiane on December 23, 2023.

Chair Shii meets with Dr. Nguyen Phu Trong, General Secretary of the Communist Party of Vietnam, in Hanoi on December 26, 2023.

high praise for the Diplomatic Vision, which, they suggested, is along the same lines as ASEAN's. In Laos, which assumed the chairmanship of the ASEAN in 2024, and in Vietnam, an ASEAN member and a country with an increasing role in the international community, we had respective meetings with the leadership of the respective ruling parties, both of which mutually confirmed that they would work together to make the AOIP a suc-

Representative Questions in the Diet

Chair Shii (right) asks questions on the ASEAN centrality and Prime Minister KISHIDA Fumio (left) answers the questions at a plenary session of the House of Representatives on February 1, 2024.

cess. This is of great significance as a real commitment to moving international politics in a positive direction.

Appeal to the Government of Japan — From our remarks in the Diet sessions

We have repeatedly urged the Japanese government to adopt a "diplomatic vision" as part of Japan's foreign policy.

I myself have stressed the importance of a "diplomatic vision" four times during the past two-plus years in representative questions at plenary sessions of the House of Representatives. In his reply, Prime Minister Kishida expressed his support for the centrality of ASEAN and his strong support for the AOIP. While our party has strongly criticized the current administration's policy of a rapid and extensive military build-up, it is of importance that the Japanese government has expressed strong support for the AOIP, even in the Diet.

Overall, our party positively evaluates the Japanese government's efforts to promote the ASEAN's four areas of cooperation, including economic cooperation. That said, I would like to emphasize that if the Japanese government "strongly supports the AOIP," it should not limit itself to cooperation in four areas such as in economic cooperation, but as the government of a country with an Article 9 in its Constitution, it should also seriously put into practice the spirit of the AOIP, which is to "promote the TAC, which stipulates the peaceful settlement of disputes, as a guide for peace, throughout East Asia." I strongly urge the development of cooperation with ASEAN in "both wings" of peace creation and the four areas of cooperation, including economic cooperation.

The JCP is determined to make every effort to realize the "Diplomatic Vision" so that this direction becomes the voice of the majority of the Japanese people, and to develop cooperation with ASEAN persistently and with the countries and peoples of East Asia.

Second Proposal : Addressing the problems of Northeast Asia through diplomacy and aiming for an East-Asian peace community

The second proposal is to address the problems of Northeast Asia through diplomacy and aim for an East-Asian peace community.

Northeast Asia has unique difficulties to overcome in comparison to Southeast Asia — make a breakthrough by demonstrating the essence of diplomacy

Through the series of meetings during the tour of Southeast Asian nations late last year, we became keenly aware that Southeast Asia has a developed good habit engaging in of dialogue, but this is not the case in Northeast Asia. Why is that? Northeast Asia has unique difficulties compared to Southeast Asia.

Rivalries and divisions among the major powers, including in military matters, are alarmingly high.

The region lacks a mechanism of dialogue that includes all countries in the region.

The war on the Korean Peninsula is not yet technically over.

There is a historical issue — Japan shows no remorse for its past war of aggression and colonial rule.

Northeast Asia's unique difficulties must be resolved by Northeast Asia itself. Moreover, the only way to resolve the issues is through diplomacy. We believe that the essence of diplomacy is to find common ground to jointly address problems based on the principles of the UN Convention and international law. In addition, there must be no winner and loser, and all parties concerned should be beneficiaries.

Based on this stance, our party has been working to solve the problems affecting Northeast Asia. Today, I will explain our proposals on some of the important issues and what we have done recently to address these issues.

"For positive breakthroughs in Japan-China relations" — "JCP proposals"

The Japan-China relationship is one of the most important bilateral relationships for both sides. However, it is currently plagued by various tensions and confrontations. How can a positive breakthrough be achieved?

Three points of "common foundation" for a positive breakthrough in the situation

The JCP on March 30 of 2023 released a set of its "proposals" entitled "For positive breakthroughs in Japan-China relations", and later met with counterparts from the Japanese and Chinese governments to explain the proposals.

In formulating the "proposals", we thoroughly reexamined all the documents that Tokyo and Beijing agreed upon or confirmed in the last five decades after the normalization of diplomatic relations in 1972. We found that there are three points of "common foundation" for a positive breakthrough in the current situation.

The first point is the Joint Statement agreed upon in the 2008 Japan-China summit, which confirms, "The two sides recognize that they are partners who cooperate together and are not threats to each other."

The second is regarding the issue of the Senkaku Islands. Tokyo and Beijing in 2014 agreed on a document which states, "Both sides recognized that they had different views as to the emergence of tensions in recent years in the waters of the East China Sea, including those around the Senkaku Islands" and that they will seek to solve the issue "through dialogue and consultation."

The third point is about a regional multilateral mechanism for peace joined by Japan and China. The Japanese and Chinese governments express support for the ASEAN Outlook on the Indo-Pacific (AOIP).

Since there exist the three points of "common foundation", it is necessary to build on them and make diplomatic efforts to achieve a positive breakthrough in bilateral relations and consolidate peace and friendship. This is what the JCP "proposals" call for.

Our "proposals" were positively accepted by the governments of both countries

By setting aside our views and stances on the issue, we compiled the "proposals" that are acceptable to the two governments and are viable.

I had separate meetings with Prime Minister Kishida Fumio and Chinese Ambassador to Japan Wu Jianghao to present the JCP "proposals." It is important that they both responded positively.

When I toured Southeast Asian countries in December last year, I explained the JCP proposals to our counterparts. I was pleased that they all expressed appreciation for the proposals.

After the release of the JCP "proposals", the leaders of Japan and China held a meeting in November last year in San Francisco for the first time in a year. They reaffirmed their commitment to promote a "mutually beneficial relationship based on common strategic interests" laid out in the 2008 Japan-China joint statement. It was a positive step forward and it is important to keep promoting dialogue at all levels.

"Not becoming threats to each other" - both sides must restrain themselves from taking actions that could exacerbate tensions and confrontations

The JCP calls on the Japanese and Chinese governments, which positively evaluated our "proposals", to take the following steps.

First, in line with their stated agreement to not "be a threat to each other", the two sides should refrain from any actions fueling tensions and confrontation.

Japan should stop its moves to possess a capability to attack enemy bases, engage in a massive military buildup, and other military provocations. China should likewise stop its attempt to change the status quo in the East China Sea by force.

JCP Proposal for Positive Breakthroughs in Japan-China Relations

Chair Shii talks with PM Kishida and hands over the "JCP proposal for positive breakthroughs in Japan-China relations" in Tokyo on March 30, 2023.

Chair Shii hands over the "JCP proposal for positive breakthroughs in Japan-China relations" to Chinese Ambassador to Japan Wu Jianghao and talks with him in Tokyo on May 4, 2023.

Senkaku Islands issue — Rules should be negotiated to restrain each other from actions that could escalate the dispute

Second, regarding the Senkaku Islands issue, the JCP urges the two governments to take concrete actions to implement the 2014 agreement between Japan and China.

The JCP proposes efforts to establish a more robust "crisis management mechanism" and to create bilateral rules so that Japan and China will refrain from actions that affect peace and stability, similar to the Declaration of Conduct of the Parties in the South China Sea agreed to by ASEAN and China.

Develop a framework for peace in East Asia based on the spirit of inclusion, not exclusion

Third is the framework for peace in East Asia. The two governments, both of which support the AOIP, should pursue an inclusive framework.

Japan should refrain from building blocs aimed at excluding and encircling China. At the same time, it is not appropriate to exclude the U.S. from security frameworks in the region.

The JCP calls on the Japanese and Chinese governments to work together to further develop the East Asia Summit, which involves all countries in the region, including the U.S. and China as well as to contribute to the success of the AOIP, which seeks the creation of a region of peace in East Asia.

The JCP is determined to make every effort

to encourage Japan and China to engage in dialogue at all levels, find common ground, jointly resolve various pending issues, and nurture a relationship of peace and friendship.

Taiwan issue — Strongly urging a peaceful solution

The issue of peace and stability in the Taiwan Strait is very important as it affects peace and stability in the region and the world. Regardless of how the issue develops, the JCP demands a peaceful solution. In the process, the will of the people if freely expressed in Taiwan must be fully respected.

The JCP opposes China's use and threat of force against Taiwan. The party also opposes military involvement and intervention by Japan and the U.S. Some Japanese hawks deliberately exaggerate the Taiwan risk in order to make their case for Japan's military buildup, by saying, "The Taiwan crisis is Japan's crisis." Such bellicose narratives should be rejected because they will create a vicious spiral of military tension over the Taiwan issue and increase the risk of war, which is the least favorable outcome for all.

Korean Peninsula issue — How to shift to "peaceful resolution through dialogue"

With regard to the Korean Peninsula, in addition to the long-standing structure of conflict - the Korean War is not technically over - the situation is becoming more complex as tensions and confrontations increase.

North Korea continues its nuclear and missile development programs in violation of relevant UN Security Council resolutions. The JCP condemns this and demands that it

be stopped. On the other hand, it should be pointed out that the United States, Japan, and South Korea are accelerating the vicious spiral of increasing military tensions by regularly holding large-scale and highly provocative joint military exercises.

It is urgently necessary for the international community to change course from further escalation of the vicious spiral of military confrontation to a "peaceful solution through dialogue" regarding the Korean peninsula issue. To this end, the JCP makes the following four recommendations.

Every effort should be made to open dialogue channels to stop the escalation of tensions

First, in order to stop the escalation of tensions, every effort should be made to open dialogue channels between the U.S. and North Korea, South and North Korea, and Japan and North Korea.

Regarding the U.S.-North Korea and South-North Korea relations, there are agreements confirmed in a series of summits in 2018 and there is the 2002 Japan-North Korea Pyongyang Declaration concerning bilateral relations. The JCP calls on the parties concerned to build on these achievements and make diplomatic efforts to resume dialogue. In this regard, we pay attention to the report that Japanese and North Korean officials have been in contact since last year.

Denuclearize the peninsula and build peace structure in integrated and phased manner — based on lessons learned in 2018-19

Second is about principles on how to promote

JCP Request on Korean Peninsula Issue

Chair Shii and Secretary Head KOIKE Akira hold talks after handing over the written request calling on the Six Parties to work for the denuclearization of the Korean Peninsula and the building of a peace structure in an integrated and phased manner to then Prime Minister ABE Shinzo to resolve the North Korean nuclear and missile issues in Tokyo on April 9, 2018.

dialogue and negotiation.

On April 6, 2018, the JCP issued a written "petition to the six parties concerned", entitled, "JCP calls for efforts to denuclearize Korean Peninsula and build peace structure in integrated and phased manner" in response to reports about the planned South-North Korea and U.S.-North Korea summit meetings. After that, important joint documents were produced in the South-North Korea summit held on April 27 and the U.S.-North Korea summit on June 12. Unfortunately, however, efforts to implement the agreements contained in the documents were later stopped and the situation took a negative turn. By studying the whole process, the JCP drew lessons from it — when considering future dialogue and negotiations, the following two principles put forward in the "petition to the six parties concerned" are very important.

The first is to promote the denuclearization of the Korean Peninsula and the establishment of a peace structure in Northeast Asia in an integrated and comprehensive manner.

Some argue that given the development of North Korea's nuclear and missile capabilities, it is necessary to recognize North Korea as a "de facto nuclear power" and negotiate nuclear disarmament with it. However, this is a dangerous argument that goes against the spirit of the Treaty on the Prohibition of Nuclear Weapons and may lead to the collapse of the nuclear non-proliferation regime. The denuclearization of the Korean peninsula should remain the ultimate goal of dialogue and negotiations among the parties concerned.

At the same time, to promote denuclearization, it is essential to end the Korean War and other hostilities, establish a regional peace structure, and resolve the security concerns of North Korea and other parties involved. It can only be achieved if the two tasks are carried out simultaneously and in an integrated manner.

In addition, in doing so, they should discuss and agree on what items need to be implemented and take a step-by-step approach to reach the goal. This is the realistic way.

Given the high level of mutual distrust, denuclearization and the establishment of a peace structure cannot be achieved overnight, even though they are the agreed goals. The only realistic approach is to make a steady progress by reducing mutual distrust and gradually building trust without haste through a step-by-step approach.

In this regard, it is significant that the 2005 Joint Statement of the Six-Party Talks states, "The Six Parties agreed to take coordinated steps to implement the afore-mentioned consensus in a phased manner in line with the principle of 'commitment for commitment, action for action'."

Japan-DPRK relations — Comprehensive resolution of various issues based on the Japan-DPRK Pyongyang Declaration

Third, the Japan-North Korea relationship is different from those of the U.S.-North Korea and South-North Korea because Japan and North Korea are not at war. On the other hand, North Korea is the only country that Japan has yet to complete postwar actions–post-colonial reconciliation. This problem must be resolved. Keeping these facts in mind, the Japanese government should take the lead in achieving a breakthrough in the situation.

Better relations between Japan and North Korea are urgently needed to resolve the issue of Japanese citizens abducted by North Korea in the past, a time-sensitive international human rights issue, and to improve relations between the U. S. and North Korea and between the two Koreas, as well as establish

peace and security in the region. It is necessary to comprehensively resolve the outstanding issues of nuclear and missile development, abduction and colonial history, and work to normalize diplomatic relations on the basis of the 2002 Japan-North Korea Pyongyang Declaration.

Based on the achievements of the Six-Party Talks, create a framework by the six parties for a solution

Fourth, the Six-Party Talks on the resolution of the North Korea issue has not been held since its sixth meeting in 2007. This multilateral framework is the most reasonable scheme for the resolution of the issue and its importance is emphasized by UN Security Council resolutions.

The JCP calls for greater efforts to resume bilateral talks and negotiations between the U.S. and North Korea, South and North Korea and Japan and North Korea, and to establish a framework for the resolution of the issues by the six countries on the basis of the 2005 joint statement and other achievements of the Six-Party Talks.

Resolving historical issues — What kind of a basic stance should Japan take 80 years after World War II?

I would like to discuss some historical issues. How Japan confronts its past wars of aggression and colonial rule is an unavoidable issue in the development of harmonious relations of peace, friendship and cooperation between Japan and other Asian countries. Next year, 2025, will mark 80 years since the end of World War II. Towards this milestone year, I would like to propose the following points as the basic stance that Japan should take.

Uphold the core contents of the three key documents of the 1990s and take appropriate actions in accordance with them

In the 1990s, the Japanese government revealed "three key documents" on historical issues. There were the 1995 "Murayama statement", which expressed remorse for "colonial rule and aggression"; the 1993 "Kono statement", which acknowledged military involvement and coercion in the Japanese military use and abuse of so-called "comfort women" and expressed remorse; and the 1998 Japan-South Korea partnership declaration, in which Japan expressed remorse and apologized for South Korean people for its colonial rule. These "three important documents" have been recognized both domestically and internationally as showing the Japanese government's progress in understanding historical issues.

However, the Abe statement, issued in the 70th year since the end of World War II, was characterized by a serious reversal from the "three key documents", such as glorifying the Japanese-Russo War, which led to the colonization of Korea, and regarding historical issues as having already been resolved. On the occasion of the 80th anniversary of the end of the war, we call for a reckoning with this retrogression, inheriting the core contents of the "three key documents" and taking appropriate action accordingly.

Yasukuni Shrine — Establish a rule that the Prime Minister, Cabinet members, and senior officers of the Self-Defense Forces are not allowed to visit the shrine in an official capacity

Yasukuni shrine was once regarded as a spiritual pillar for mobilizing the people for the war on aggression, and for politicians in the national political arena to visit the Yasukuni Shrine means to signify their affirmation of the war of aggression. Pilgrimages to Yasukuni Shrine by senior officers of the SDF not only contravene the "separation of religion and state", but also are a dangerous reversal of the continuity with the former Japanese military. We call for the establishment of a rule in Japanese politics that, at the very least, visits to Yasukuni Shrine by the Prime Minister, Cabinet ministers and senior officers of the SDF should not take place.

Japanese military "comfort women" and "forced laborers" issues — Restore the honor and dignity of all victims

Although the Japanese and South Korean governments have taken certain measures, the issue of Japanese military "comfort women" has not been resolved. At the root of this lies Japan's unwillingness to express remorse for its past mistakes in its own words. In the case of the "forced laborers" issue, neither the Japanese government nor the companies concerned have apologized to the victims or expressed remorse. This is combined with an unwillingness to regard the issue as a serious violation of human rights linked to colonial rule.

We call for a fundamental change in this

attitude and the fulfilment of political responsibility until the honor and dignity of all victims is restored.

Standing on the right side of history, we must make a fundamental reckoning with the war of aggression and the illegal and unjust colonial rule

During this time, there has been a growing movement on a global scale to trace back the responsibility for colonial rule and slavery and to demand an apology. The Durban Declaration, adopted at an international conference hosted by the United Nations in 2001, declares, "wherever and whenever it [colonialism] occurred, it must be condemned and its reoccurrence prevented". Twenty years later now, human history has shown great progress in this regard. Standing on the right side of world history, Japan must make a fundamental reckoning with the war of aggression and its illegal and unjust colonial rule.

The JCP, as a party with a history of risking its members' lives to oppose past wars of aggression and colonial rule, expressed its determination to do its utmost to achieve a reasoned resolution of historical issues.

Pursue the "Initiative for Peace and Cooperation in Northeast Asia" as a major goal

As mentioned above, we reiterate our call for building on efforts to resolve the various problems in Northeast Asia through dialogue, and for making efforts to advance the "habit of dialogue" in Northeast Asia while creating an inclusive framework for peace and aiming for the conclusion of a Treaty of Amity and Cooperation (TAC) in Northeast Asia.

The JCP has proposed the "Initiative for Peace and Cooperation in Northeast Asia" at the 26th Party Congress in 2014, calling for the establishment of an inclusive peace framework in Northeast Asia based on the TAC. We will pursue this initiative as a major goal.

Only when this comes to fruition will Southeast Asia and Northeast Asia be linked by a Treaty of Amity and Cooperation and an East Asian Peace Community can be created.

The problems facing Northeast Asia are daunting, and some people may be skeptical that they can be resolved through diplomacy. However, when ASEAN was initially established, Southeast Asia was in the midst of even more tension, conflict and warfare than Northeast Asia is today, and ASEAN has successfully created a regional community of peace through more than half a century of persistent efforts at dialogue and cooperation. There is no reason why Southeast Asia can do it and Northeast Asian cannot, so let us learn from ASEAN's experience and work together with ASEAN countries to make Northeast Asia a war-free region like Southeast Asia.

Third Proposal : Solutions based on the UN Charter and international law for Gaza crisis and aggression against Ukraine

The third proposal is to resolve the Gaza crisis and the aggression against Ukraine solely on the basis of the UN Charter and international law.

This is a major issue that is also closely related to the creation of peace in East Asia.

Stop genocide in Gaza — Seek a just solution to the Palestinian question

As a result of Israel's massive offensive, the Palestinians in Gaza are facing an extreme humanitarian disaster, with over 33,000 confirmed deaths and widespread starvation. While Hamas's indiscriminate attack and hostage taking on October 7 are unacceptable, Israel must not use them as an excuse to commit genocide against Palestinians in Gaza. The JCP strongly urges Israel to immediately cease its onslaught and to accept an immediate ceasefire, and urges the U.S. to end its military support and fulfil its responsibility to curb Israel's lawlessness.

The violation of the Palestinian people's right to self-determination, the prolonged expansion of the occupation, and the continuing gross injustice of Israeli brutality going unpunished are a grave reversal of peace and justice in Asia region and the world.

The JCP strongly calls for the international community to take action for a just solution to the Palestinian problem based on the three principles of (1) Israel's withdrawal from the occupied Palestinian territories, (2) realization of the right to self-determination which includes the Palestinians' right to establish an independent state, and (3) creation of mutual recognition to respect the right to coexistence.

How to end the war against Ukraine and restore peace and stability in Europe

The world's overwhelming majority of nations need to unite behind the single-minded goal of upholding the UN Charter

Two years have passed since the start of Russia's aggression against Ukraine, with no end to the war in sight. Needless to say, the responsibility for the war lies with Russia which continues its unlawful aggression in violation of the UN Charter. The JCP strongly calls for the immediate and total withdrawal of Russian military troops.

At the same time, it must be pointed out that there are weaknesses in the U.S. response. One is that the Biden administration is pushing the slogan "democracy vs autocracy", and imposing an argument bringing division into the world based on "values". Another is that the U.S. has adopted a "double standard", condemning Russia's aggression against Ukraine but defending Israel's attack on Gaza, which violates international law. I would like to emphasize that overcoming these weaknesses and uniting the overwhelming majority of the international community on the single point of "upholding the UN Charter" is the way to end war.

The importance of reinvigorating the Organization for Security and Cooperation in Europe (OSCE), even if it is difficult

There is a movement to use this issue as a pretext for a major military build-up, claiming, "Ukraine is tomorrow's East Asia", which the JCP opposes. In Europe, the OSCE has developed an inclusive peace framework in which all European countries including Russia, participate. However, the functioning of the OSCE was not well utilized, leading to "power against power" rivalry and division, which became the background for the war. This course of events shows the importance of developing an inclusive peace framework that embraces all countries in the region as a priority for security, as ASEAN is currently doing, instead of falling into rivalry and division based on an exclusive framework.

The UN General Assembly resolution calling for Russia's immediate withdrawal from Ukraine in October 2022 calls for international and regional organizations including the OSCE to support a peaceful resolution of the conflict through "political dialogue, negotiation, mediation, and other peaceful means." I believe that the reactivation of the OSCE, even if that may be extremely difficult, will be important in ending Russia's war against Ukraine and restoring peace and stability in Europe.

A call for national and civic movements to create peace in East Asia

In three respects, I have made proposals for creating peace in East Asia, but in order to bring this to fruition, it is necessary not only for governments to work together but also for the participation of national and civic movements. In Northeast Asia and Southeast Asia, the peoples of both regions want peace. Real peace can only be created if grassroots movements of the general populace support it.

Lessons learned from efforts made to establish the Treaty on the Prohibition of Nuclear Weapons

We have learned this deeply from the process leading to the formation of the Treaty on the Prohibition of Nuclear Weapons (TPNW). The TPNW would not have been possible without the strong efforts by the civil society movement, led by atomic bomb survivors (Hibakusha). The JCP sent party delegations twice to the UN Conference on the TPNW in 2017, delivered speeches at the UN Conference, and put our efforts into establishing the treaty. We saw firsthand how powerful civil society can be, and especially, what a significant contribution the Hibakusha's activities made.

I believe that the great task of building peace in East Asia can only be achieved through the joint efforts made by governments, political parties, and civil society.

Tokyo rally to commemorate the 76th anniversary of the enforcement of the post-war pacifist Constitution on May 3, 2023.

歴史的な核兵器禁止条約を採択

歴史的条約を力に、核兵器全面廃絶の実現を
——核兵器禁止条約の採択を心から歓迎する

日本共産党 幹部会委員長 志位 和夫

国連会議

加盟国約3分の2 122カ国

Gender equality at the core of peacebuilding

In this context, I would like to emphasize the integrated pursuit of gender equality and peace. "Peace" is one of the common starting points for the founding of women's organizations in Japan that have consistently fought for the elimination of discrimination against women since the end of World War II. Women played a very significant role in the birth of the TPNW. We would like to continue our struggle with realization of gender equality at the heart of peace creation.

I conclude my speech by sincerely calling on people at home and abroad to engage in various forms of national and civic movements to help create peace in East Asia, and sincerely hoping that the JCP's proposals will be a small step in advancing this. Thank you.

ISBN978-4-88048-095-4

C0031 ¥800E

定価　本体800円 (税別)

東アジアの平和構築への提言
——ASEANと協力して

Proposals for Peace Creation in East Asia
In Cooperation with ASEAN

2024年7月10日　第1刷発行

発売　ジャパン・プレス・サービス

〒151-0051　東京都渋谷区千駄ヶ谷4-25-6

電話：03-3423-2381

ファクス：03-3423-2383

電子メール：info@japan-press.co.jp

印刷・製本：株式会社 光陽メディア

落丁、乱丁がありましたらお取り替えいたします。